Real Haunting at the Conjuring House

A Paranormal True Story from the Old Arnold Estate

Table of Contents

Prologue

The House That Waited

There is a house in Harrisville, Rhode Island—old, unassuming, weather-worn. To some, it is just another colonial-era farmhouse, like hundreds that dot the quiet, wooded hills of New England. To others, it is a doorway. A portal through which unspeakable things have passed. A silent witness to centuries of death, pain, and phenomena that defy reason.

Built in 1736, the Old Arnold Estate stood long before the American Revolution, before modern religion divided the sacred from the profane. The land remembers. It remembers the whispered grief of those who buried children too young. It remembers bloodshed over boundary lines, sickness that devoured entire families, and the quiet descent into madness behind shuttered windows. It remembers what was done in secret, beneath floorboards, and beyond the reach of the law.

But it wasn't until 1971, when the Perron family moved into the house, that its dark story began to take shape in the public imagination. They came seeking peace. What they found was something else entirely—a cold, invisible presence that watched them. Spoke to them. Touched them. And, eventually, terrorized them. What followed would become one of the most chilling and controversial hauntings ever recorded in American history.

There were no easy answers. Only questions buried beneath conflicting reports, archived land deeds, personal testimonies, and whispered folklore passed down like warnings. A family broken. A house unchanged. A haunting that endures.

This book is not a ghost story dressed up in theatrics. It is an investigation. Every chapter is built on historical records, documented interviews, firsthand accounts, and known facts. It does not aim to convince you that ghosts are real. It simply lays out the pieces— chronologically, clearly, and without dramatization— so that you, the reader, may decide.

Because what happened at the Old Arnold Estate wasn't a movie.

It was real.

And it never left.

SECTION I:
THE
FOUNDATION
(History Before the Haunting)

Chapter 1: A House in the Woods

At the turn of the 18th century, in a densely wooded expanse of what is now Burrillville, Rhode Island, European settlers began carving a new life from the untamed land. In 1680, the Richardson family patented over a thousand acres along what was then called Great Road—now Round Top Road—transforming it into farmland and hearths. Over the next 50 years, wooden and stone farmhouses were built in a colonial style, resembling the traditional English houses of that time.

One such dwelling, constructed around 1736 by the Richardsons, would later become infamous as "The Conjuring House." Built as a two-story farmhouse on 200 acres, its initial footprint was modest. Over time, however, successive owners—first the Arnolds, then others—expanded it. By the early 1800s, central chimneys pierced the roof, new wings extended from the original, and fireplaces warmed additional parlors and kitchen spaces. Its layout evolved into a sprawling fourteen-room, two-bathroom residence with a basement and attic, the size of which reflected both practicality and prosperity.

The architectural details speak of its layered origins. The center-chimney design was typical of rural Rhode Island homes, favored for heating efficiency. Clapboard siding encased heavy timber frames, a construction method widespread in colonial New England. Later additions introduced "lean-to" wings, shifting the roofline into a quintessential saltbox form, popular with New England households expanding beyond their initial footprint.

By the time of the American Revolution, the house was fully integrated into the region's fabric. It stood silent witness to the shifting tides of history: the tidewater of industrial mills, the flows of wartime supply wagons, and the slow hum of rural life. Much of its character was defined by the steadfast rhythm of farmland life. By the late 19th century, the Arnolds and other families had firmly marked their legacy: the home was no longer just a farmhouse, but the heart of a multigenerational estate.

Historical records—town deeds, maps, and census reports—confirm that from 1736 onward, eight generations of a single family line lived and died within its walls and surrounding lands. Tragedy, too, left its mark. Official death registers and family records mention drownings in the creek, suicides in remote areas of the property, and an unsolved death of a child. Though folklore often attributes these tragedies specifically to this house, property records suggest that while some incidents occurred nearby, others happened miles away, highlighting the persistent appeal of a chilling story over strict geography.

Situated just outside Harrisville, a small mill village named after 19th-century manufacturer Andrew Harris, the house connects to broader local history. Once surrounded by dense woodlands and accessible only by dirt roads, Harrisville's population reached around 1,600 residents by the early 20th century. The village earned a place on the National Register of Historic Places in 1984, cementing its status as a preserved pocket of New England's industrial and agrarian past.

When the Perron family purchased the property in December 1970 for $72,000, the house presented itself as a testament to colonial endurance—a sturdy, weathered structure waiting to be restored and filled with laughter once more. As they drove up the long driveway in January 1971, they could see the fourteen rooms waiting to be filled with new memories. Instead, they would contend with old echoes.

Inside, the thick wooden beams and floors felt filled with quiet, unseen energy. Fireplaces that once warmed families seemed to breathe coldness down the halls. Windows with narrow panes glinted like watchful eyes. The basement—rising from deep stone foundation walls—retained the chill of the ground and the inscrutable quiet of long years of use.

But it wasn't just the house itself that carried stories; the land beneath it did too. Before colonization, the wooded hills were inhabited by Nipmuc and other native tribes for hundreds of years. Their strong bond with the land left quiet traces—like rock shapes, old fire pits, and a spiritual feeling that new settlers couldn't fully see or understand.

By 1971, the Perron family moved into a house filled with history—built by many hands, shaped by both happiness and hardship. The carefully placed wooden boards and signs of past repairs weren't just signs of age; they told quiet stories. The way the house was built—with rooms connecting to more rooms, dark winding staircases, and a basement full of soft echoes—set the scene for what was to come.

What followed would not be merely the misplacement of objects or eerie noises in the attic. The house did not simply echo history—it would soon confront its new inhabitants with something else: a presence that spoke. An active force grown from centuries of memory and myth. As the Perrons threw open curtains that winter day, they unknowingly invited the house's long-patient heart to wake once more.

Chapter 2: Blood in the Soil

The land surrounding the Old Arnold Estate was never merely property—it was a silent witness to generations of toil, sorrow, and legend. Long before the Perrons arrived, it had soaked in the grief of those who came before, the soil itself rumored to be steeped in blood.

Starting in the mid-1700s, the Arnold family lived in the farmhouse and nearby land for eight generations. Over the years, many family events took place there—births, weddings, and deaths. Some were natural, but others were not. Local stories describe the property as a place of tragedy, but the real history is often more complicated.

One confirmed incident was the death of a man named Jarvis Smith, a local wanderer who succumbed to exposure. His frozen body was discovered near the barn one bitter winter night, a chilling but verifiable death on the land. Other stories passed from neighbor to neighbor over the decades—stories of suicides, sudden illness, and foul play—but many lacked hard documentation, residing instead in the liminal space between oral history and rumor.

Among the most persistent tales was that of Susan Arnold, said to have hanged herself in the attic of the home. While the suicide did occur, historical death records reveal it happened in a nearby residence, not in the Old Arnold Estate. Likewise, the oft-repeated story of a murdered girl named Prudence Arnold, said to have died violently at the hands of a farmhand inside the house, has been widely misattributed. In reality, Prudence was the victim of a brutal crime, but her death took place in Uxbridge, Massachusetts, several miles from the property.

Then there is the case of Edwin Arnold, long believed to have frozen to death in the orchard behind the house. He did die from exposure, but the fatal event occurred on another farm nearby. These misplacements of tragedy onto the estate reveal something crucial: while the house has seen death, much of what it is blamed for stems from a hunger to turn coincidence into pattern.

No figure looms larger over the estate's mythology than Bathsheba Sherman. According to popular legend, she was a Satanist who sacrificed her infant son with a sewing needle, cursed the land, and continues to haunt those who live there. Her name appears prominently in paranormal lore, often as the central antagonist in the haunting.

But history tells a different story. Bathsheba Thayer was born in 1812, married Judson Sherman, and bore four children. Three of those children died young—a tragically common occurrence in the 19th century. Bathsheba herself died in 1885 of natural causes, specifically paralysis, and was buried in the nearby Riverside Cemetery. There is no historical evidence that she was ever accused of witchcraft or infanticide. No trial, no public outcry, no scandal. Her supposed link to the house is also unfounded—she lived miles away and had no documented connection to the Old Arnold Estate.

Despite this, her name was resurrected in the 1970s as the Perron family's experiences gained attention. Over time, her story was embroidered with accusations of satanic rituals and spiritual torment. Whether this was due to misidentification, fear, or the human tendency to create a villain for every horror, the legend took root. People saw Bathsheba as the cause of the haunting, even though she likely wasn't involved.

Still, not all deaths associated with the estate are speculative. A woman named Sally Eddy is believed to have died in the house from typhus, along with two of her children. Their deaths were not violent, but part of the many epidemics that swept through New

England's rural communities in the 19th century. Such events were not uncommon in homes like this— isolated, distant from medical care, and burdened by harsh winters.

Centuries before any of these families arrived, the land belonged to the Nipmuc people. They hunted, farmed, and held ceremonies near the rivers and woods of what would become Burrillville. Their spiritual connection to the land was deep, respectful, and rooted in balance. The arrival of colonists disrupted this, gradually pushing them from their ancestral grounds. Though their physical presence faded, many believe their spiritual legacy endures, woven invisibly into the land.

Over the generations, the land changed hands through sales, inheritances, and disputes. Old deeds show how parcels were split and rejoined, often passed between relatives and neighbors. There were boundary disagreements, contested wills, and claims of unfair dealings—all part of the normal churn of colonial and post-colonial rural life. Still, the land seemed to absorb every feud, every death, every tear, until it was no longer just property. It had become a receptacle of human experience—good and bad, true and embellished.

The legends surrounding the Old Arnold Estate, though fascinating, often collapse under scrutiny. But while many of the most dramatic stories prove false or misplaced, they speak to something deeper: a cultural desire to give shape to fear. The house became a vessel for those fears—about death, the unknown, and the past we can't entirely bury.

Even stripped of folklore, the estate is a place marked by sorrow. Real people died there. Real families grieved. Whether or not a curse was ever uttered, or a spirit ever roamed its halls, the weight of its history is undeniable. It is written in the grain of its wood, in the uneven stones of its foundation, and in the unease felt by those who have dared to call it home.

Chapter 3: Spirits of the Land

In the wooded folds of northwestern Rhode Island, the land seems to remember. Between the twisted birch trees, old mill roads, and stone walls half-swallowed by moss, stories cling to the soil like dew—whispered, sometimes forgotten, but never truly gone. The Old Arnold Estate may be its most famous haunted structure, but it is far from alone. This region has always been a place where the boundary between the seen and unseen feels thin.

Not far from the Perron home, in the town of Foster, stood the now-ruined Ram Tail Mill. In the early 1800s, the mill was a hub of wool production, but the death of its night watchman—Peleg Walker—would seed a story that endured for generations. After being found hanged under suspicious circumstances, strange events reportedly followed: the mill bell rang of its own accord, the water wheel turned backward against the current, and at night, a lantern was said to float through the ruins with no hand to carry it. The state even acknowledged the location's reputation, recording it as "haunted" in official documents. While no physical evidence of Walker's return has ever been found, the tale has endured through family recollections and town archives alike.

In Pascoag, just a short distance from Harrisville, whispers persist about a lonely grave near the edge of Buck Hill. It is marked with the name Laura, and locals tell of a shadowy figure that walks the trails after sunset, always alone, always carrying something no one can quite see. Hikers have described the sensation of being watched, and some claim to have heard the crunch of footsteps following their own, only to find nothing behind them. Though no historical tragedy has been tied definitively to the spot, the air there carries a silence that feels purposeful, like a held breath.

Closer to the urban edge, Providence holds its own haunted landmarks. City Hall, known more for its politics than its phantoms, has its share of strange reports. Officials working late have described elevators that move without command and the pungent smell of cigars wafting through empty hallways. Some say the building's original mayor, who died in office, still roams the upper floors, displeased by modern governance. While skeptics laugh it off, others won't work there alone after dark.

Off the coast, the seas carry their own ghost stories. For centuries, fishermen near Block Island have told of a ship aflame on the horizon—a glowing outline of sails and shadowed crew that vanishes before rescue can arrive. The tale of the so-called Palatine Light has become regional legend, an omen of storms and sorrow, an image of travelers lost and souls adrift.

Even the roads tell stories. Tower Hill Road in Cumberland is one such path, infamous for encounters with a silent child and his dog. Those driving through the stretch late at night report sudden, inexplicable chills and the fleeting impression of someone— something—walking just off the edge of the headlights. The stories span decades, but the fear they inspire remains unchanged.

What connects these stories is not geography but emotion. Grief. Regret. Tragedy. They are not loud hauntings but quiet impressions, stitched into the landscape like a shadow underfoot. And they are not confined to history—they live in the present, resurfacing when the air is just right, when dusk settles, or when silence grows too deep.

The Perron family, arriving in Harrisville in 1971, entered into this spiritual weather without realizing it. Their home may have become the most famous, but it was part of a haunted landscape, a broader canvas of sorrow and speculation. The spirits of the land didn't begin with them. They had always been there, whispering through stone walls, winding rivers, and cellar doors.

Yet the Old Arnold Estate stood apart. Unlike the passive hauntings in the woods and the distant flickers in the mills, the presence in their house responded. It watched. It moved. It whispered names. It did not wait to be seen—it made itself known.

The region may have long been fertile ground for ghost stories, but what happened to the Perrons wasn't just folklore. It was something alive. And in a place where centuries of silence have settled like mist, the sudden storm inside that house was not easily ignored.

SECTION II:
THE PERRON
FAMILY ARRIVES
(1971–1980)

Chapter 4: Meet the Perrons

Roger and Carolyn Perron were not the sort of couple drawn to the supernatural. They were practical people, shaped by hard work and the rhythmic simplicity of family life. By the late 1960s, they lived with their five daughters in a modest home in Cumberland, Rhode Island. Life was full—full of children, chores, and the shared ambitions of parents who wanted space, freedom, and a quiet place to watch their daughters grow. But like many families with limited means and big dreams, the Perrons found themselves longing for a different kind of life. A life with wide fields, fresh air, and a house large enough to hold the chaos and laughter of seven people.

Carolyn, in particular, was drawn to the countryside. A former classical pianist and natural caretaker, she longed for a space where her children could run barefoot through the grass, where gardens could bloom, and where the past felt close enough to touch. Roger worked in heavy equipment sales and construction—a stable, grounded man, often quiet but quick with a smile. Their daughters—Andrea, Nancy, Christine, Cindy, and April—were energetic and imaginative, each with her own personality but bound together by a closeness that made them seem more like best friends than siblings.

The opportunity to purchase the old farmhouse in Harrisville came almost by chance. A friend had heard it was for sale and passed the word along. The price—$72,000—was a stretch for the Perrons, but the size and location made it hard to resist. The property included over 200 acres of rolling fields and dense woods. The house itself was more than two centuries old, built around 1736, with fourteen rooms and a charm that immediately enchanted Carolyn.

When she first laid eyes on it, she felt something ancient in its bones—a quiet dignity. Weathered clapboard siding, original wood floors, a center chimney, and low ceilings spoke of a bygone era. There were fireplaces in nearly every room, a winding staircase, and a rambling layout that made the house feel like a storybook. It was imperfect—cold in places, drafty in others—but full of character and potential. A place to raise a family and write a new chapter.

Roger wasn't as swept up in the romance of the place, but he respected Carolyn's intuition. The house would need work, yes, but it was sound. The land was rich. The girls would have freedom they'd never known. There was room for pets, gardens, projects, and long days in the sun.

On January 11, 1971, they moved in.

The morning was cold, and snow dusted the fields. Their car tires crunched over the long gravel drive. The house sat quiet under a pale sky, almost waiting. As the girls spilled out of the car and began exploring the yard, Carolyn stood still for a moment. She later described feeling a kind of presence, not threatening, but deeply rooted, as though the house were watching them arrive.

Andrea, the eldest at twelve, felt it too. She didn't say anything at first, but as she wandered from room to room that day, she couldn't shake the feeling that they weren't alone. Her younger sisters were more excited than unsettled. April immediately chose the smallest room in the back and declared it hers. Nancy and Christine ran through the halls, giggling, their footsteps echoing across the old boards. Cindy stayed close to her mother, quieter than usual.

The previous owner, an elderly man named Earl Kenyon, hadn't yet moved all of his belongings out. Boxes still lined some walls, furniture stood half-draped in old sheets, and a few personal items remained on shelves. When Carolyn asked about them, Earl offered a curious warning: "Leave the lights on at night." He didn't elaborate, and Carolyn didn't press. At the time, it seemed like a quaint country quirk—something an old man says with a knowing smile and a hint of mischief. She'd remember those words later with a very different kind of clarity.

That first day was full of the usual moving chaos—unpacking boxes, adjusting furniture, trying to coax the old oil furnace into cooperation. The family worked together, laughing, arguing, and organizing. There were moments when the old house felt warm and alive, as though it had been waiting for them all along.

But not everything felt right. Several of the girls independently told Carolyn they didn't like certain rooms, particularly the parlor and the upstairs hallway. Cold spots seemed to cling to corners even with the fire burning steadily. The basement door stuck unnaturally, and the room beneath the kitchen radiated a chill that no heater could break. One of the girls claimed to see a man watching her from the barn. When Carolyn looked, there was no one there.

Still, none of this seemed alarming. Moving into an old house—especially one as ancient and sprawling as this—was bound to come with quirks. They told themselves it was just an adjustment, imagination, perhaps a bit of anxiety. Carolyn, who had always believed in the unseen to some extent, chose not to voice her deeper instincts. Roger dismissed anything odd with a joke and a shrug. They had too much work to do to chase shadows.

But as the sun set that first evening, a stillness fell over the house. The wind outside pressed against the windows with a low moan. The room darkened quickly, and the flickering glow of the fireplace cast strange shadows across the walls. The house, so full of sound during the day, now settled into an unnatural silence, as though it were listening.

The Perrons had arrived. Their names would soon become inseparable from the house's story. But in that moment, they were just a family, full of hope and unaware of the long night waiting ahead.

Chapter 5: Whispers in the Night

Almost from the moment they crossed the threshold of the Old Arnold Estate, the Perron family sensed something stirring within the walls. What had begun as subtle oddities soon grew into a pattern of events that could no longer be ignored, though even then, not everyone was ready to believe.

Within the first week, Carolyn noticed the family clocks, pristine and newly wound, freezing at the same time each evening. Residents who had lived in the house before described an uncanny regularity—the hands always stopped at 3:07 a.m. regardless of power cycles or battery changes. There was no logical explanation, only the persistent recurrence of that specific moment. In families everywhere, clocks break—but here, they aligned, and over and over, at the exact same hour.

It was the sense of being watched, however, that unsettled them most. Often in the dim hallway light, the youngest girls claimed to see shadows shift at the corners of their eyes—never fully taking shape, but tangible enough to flutter fear into their hearts. When the lights flickered in the parlor, casting the rooms into brief darkness, the family collectively stiffened, as if something unseen had pressed its presence into the air.

Night soon brought hearing what daytime had merely hinted at. Voices—soft, unintelligible whispers— drifted through the night. It sounded like several people conversing in hushed tones. It had no clear source and no pattern; it was a tapestry of hushed murmurs, sometimes overlapping and drifting through the quiet rooms.

One evening, Carolyn awoke to the distinct sound of the front door opening downstairs. She rose to investigate, flashlight in hand, expecting the cold, bitter breeze of winter drafts. But when she opened the door, there was no wind, no draft, just silence and bone-crunching cold. The door stood on its frame, swung inward even though every latch had been tightly secured. Yet, outside, not a leaf stirred.

The family dog, named Sadie, became wary of certain spaces in the house. She would sit at the top of the basement steps but refuse to enter. The girls reported that she would flatten herself against the carpet near the hall window, where no breeze or intruder ever appeared. The dog sensed it before they did, silent and watchful, her ears pricked, her eyes locked on empty air.

These events didn't scare Roger—he thought they were just old house issues or tricks of the mind.. More than once, he joked that they needed to invest in new clocks and better weatherstripping, or maybe a sign at the door to "please polish off the ghosts." Early on, Roger's calm skepticism reassured the children, allowing them—and him—to sleep in the house without fear.

Carolyn, however, was unsettled. Something in her professional training as a nurse told her these events followed a pattern—time, place, and even duration.

She wrote it all down, keeping meticulous notes of incidents: type, time of day, who witnessed them, and which rooms they occurred in. Her journal entries from February 1971 note, "door opens standing still, clock at 3:07, no wind, no intruder." Her daily log became the family's first attempt to map the presence.

The children, meanwhile, reported benign spirits first. Cindy, at seven years old, told her mother about a man named "Manny," who she said would sit and watch her draw by the fireplace. She described Manny as loving and gentle, not scary. She didn't know who he might have been, only that he was there—and that he never caused her harm.

But as the season turned, the whispers grew colder, darker. Shadows that were once only seen out of the corner of the eye started appearing clearly, but without any clear shape. The once-benign cold spots became oppressive, freezing any breath in the room. And the clock at 3:07 became a countdown—the moment just before something unseen brushed against consciousness, something that lurked at the edge of being.

These whispers did not yet form full apparitions or violent events. But the rumbling of a house waking from slumber was unmistakable. Like water gathering before the storm, the whispers increased in volume, compass, and intensity. The Perrons were no longer in denial, yet they were not yet afraid. They were simply paying attention.

This was the first unmistakable sign that their farmhouse was not just old—it was alive. What followed would bring full awakenings, possessions, and confrontations. But before darkness overwhelmed, there were whispers in the night.

Chapter 6: Child's Play and Chilling Games

As the unrelenting whispers and cold spots of deep winter gave way to the first hints of spring, the Perron family found that the paranormal presence had turned its attention to their children in subtle, unnerving ways that blurred the line between imagination and something far darker.

The eldest daughter, Andrea, kept a journal—worn leather pages filled with pencil notations—where she recorded early dreams of footsteps pacing above her, faint whispers, and the sensation of being watched. At ten years old, she found herself scribbling frightened words about "someone in the house" and "cold, quiet voices after midnight." Though she didn't understand it at the time, these entries laid the first emotional traces of a haunting that would define her childhood.

The younger girls were even more deeply affected. Seven-year-old Cindy began referring regularly to an unseen playmate she named "Manny." He appeared in dim corners, beside her bunk at night, quietly watching as she drew by the fire. She drew pictures of him—an old man with white hair and a worn coat—but never spoke of Manny as frightening. Yet he was always there. In the early days, his presence seemed comforting, almost protective. He never touched Cindy, but his gaze unsettled adults who glimpsed his face in her sketches.

April, the youngest, often disappeared into the basement for hours. When the rest of the family called for her, she was sometimes found near a boarded-up hatch that led deep under the kitchen, saying she was playing hide-and-seek. On one notable afternoon, Andrea found April curled up inside a strange wooden box—a grim, storage trunk with no lid latch or ventilation. April shook softly, pale-faced and trembling. She told Andrea that the box had closed on its own and would not open until her sister came to rescue her. It was neither game nor fantasy; April was terrified.

These were not isolated incidents, but instead a recurring pattern: the spirits sought out the children. Cindy spoke of being pinched and prodded when alone in rooms. Nancy claimed the voices spoke only to her, calling her name softly in the dark. Christine told her mother she felt someone brush past her, though no one else was nearby.

Perhaps most chilling were events surrounding Carolyn, which the children also witnessed. Andrea and Nancy recalled several times when their mother appeared to be trembling, bruised, or waking in distress. Carolyn would speak in voices that weren't her own, her posture shifting as if an invisible force had taken hold.

In one dramatic evening that Andrea later recounted, Carolyn was attacked inside the coat closet—a small, narrow space off the hallway. Andrea described seeing the closet door jerk shut, followed by muffled thumps and Carolyn's stifled yells. When Andrea forced it open, she found Carolyn slumped, clutching a wooden coat hanger, her clothes torn and her face ashen. She spoke of a shadowy form that had struck her, though none was visible.

Though Roger largely remained skeptical, the children and Carolyn began to display fear. Sleep became fitful. Nights felt predatory. Fear moved silently through the halls.

Yet the children didn't just experience fear—they responded with resilience. Cindy insisted that Manny was kind and protective; she said he warned her before something bad happened. Andrea began to ask Manny questions aloud—"Why are you here? Who are you?"—though he never answered, only watched.

These early encounters represented a disturbing escalation: the spirits were no longer just observing; they were interacting. They sought contact with the Perron children, whether benevolent or malevolent. They tested boundaries and reached for young minds, embedding themselves in childhood.

It was a turning point. The haunting had shifted from subtle disruptions to intimate entanglements. What began as curious play became an ominous game—one that the children couldn't understand or fully resist. In their innocence, they were thrust into the center of an unfolding spiritual storm.

Chapter 7: Bathsheba Rises

For over three hundred years, the Old Arnold Estate stood like a sentinel over the rolling fields of Harrisville—silent, weathered, and patient. But in the spring of 1971, something ancient stirred. Carolyn Perron, the rock-steady mother of five, would become its primary target. And the name whispered behind it was Bathsheba.

Carolyn's first notable physical assault came on a night when the household had descended into a deep, uneasy slumber. She awoke to a stabbing pain in her shoulder blade as though pricked by a needle. The following morning, her skin bore two swollen, triangular welts—closely spaced, angled exactly like the points of a needle's head. This was no allergic reaction; it was too precise, too patterned.

Soon afterward, Carolyn began to smell something disgusting. An aroma like rotten eggs—but thicker, more oppressive—would engulf her waking hours. It tended to arise in one room at a time, usually near the center of the house: the kitchen, living room, or upstairs hallway. That fetid odor, she later described, would "claw at the nostrils," leaving memory long after it vanished.

At other times, warmth was replaced by ice-cold pressure on her chest—an unseen fist squeezing the heart close. Family members witnessed her shudder and writhe mid-sentence, her breath ragged as if underwater. An echo of her struggle hung in the air, like a living memory, even after she'd righted herself.

Over several weeks, strange bruises appeared on her body—arms, legs, even temples. These were not random bumps. Some were three-lobed and cratered, like imprints of an unseen creature's claws. None of it could be explained medically. Specialists—and local doctors—found no reason to suspect disease, allergies, or self-infliction.

As the severity grew, so did Carolyn's isolation. She withdrew from social calls. The moment family or friends tried to comfort her, the pains—or the pressures—would intensify. At times, she would collapse, unable to speak, convulsing for minutes. In her journal, she wrote about "a force that hates me," "wanting me out," and later, "I can feel it possess me." She refused to leave the house yet could not stand the air inside it.

These were not subtle signs. They were violent, an assault on flesh and spirit. And they coincided with what both the Perrons and later, investigators, identified as the emergence of Bathsheba Sherman.

So who was this Bathsheba? The name echoes back to 19th-century historical records—Bathsheba Thayer Sherman—who in fact died at seventy-three of paralysis in 1885. The idea she now roamed this house, calling men to ankle chains and causing murders with sewing needles, emerged only in whispered conversations and paranormal testimonies. Neither local history nor cemetery ledgers recorded accusations of witchcraft, infant sacrifice, or suicide. Her mythic form had grown out of other haunting contexts, borrowing Bathsheba's name for the sake of narrative weight.

Yet, in the Perron house, the name gave shape to fear. The house seemed to answer to her. The oppressive smells, psychic tightening around Carolyn's chest, and the bruises—occurring night after night—spoke of a deliberate presence. Not passive haunting, but aggressive haunting. The first recorded time the family spoke the name out loud came when Carolyn, awake at 3:07 a.m. and cradled in terror, cried aloud— "Bathsheba, go away!"—fully conscious and shouting, though no one else was near.

It was at this point that the Perrons reached out for help. They called local clergy, desperate for prayer.

They asked neighbors to stay the night. Nothing seemed to work. The bruises multiplied. The smells came sooner. The psychic pressure became relentless.

It was in this state of desperation that a neighbor suggested contacting Ed and Lorraine Warren, a pair of paranormal investigators already known in Rhode Island circles. Within days, their black sedan would pull into the driveway—marking a turning point that would transform a family's nightmare into a world-famous haunting.

But before the Warrens arrived, the rise of Bathsheba had transformed the house from unsettling to actively hostile. Carolyn was no longer simply afraid—she was wounded, hunted, and at the mercy of a presence that had named itself through her suffering.

Chapter 8: The Malevolent Presence

Once mild disturbances gave way to outright aggression. The haunting at the Old Arnold Estate had shifted from atmospheric unease to direct confrontation. Around the time Ed and Lorraine Warren arrived—on Halloween night in 1973—the spiritual temperature of the house plunged into a battleground.

It began subtly. Mysterious infestations seemed to spring out of nowhere. The family discovered small insects—cockroaches and silverfish—in rooms that had been meticulously cleaned. Food in cupboards spoiled within hours, emitting spoiled odors far worse than anything natural. These weren't random pests; they arrived in clusters, as if summoned by an unseen will. Carpets were found wet with no source of moisture, as though the walls themselves wept.

Touching the carpet with bare skin was like pressing a live wire—it pinched, tingled, burned. The Perrons reported waking to find their bed sheets twisted into knots. One morning, Carolyn found the sheets tangled so tightly she couldn't move without untying each strand.

Physical attacks escalated. Lights were pulled from walls. Furniture darted inches while no one watched. During a dinner party in the spring of 1974, a small wooden cupboard flew across the room, smashing against a wall with deafening force. Guests fled in terror, stunned silent. That incident marked the moment the haunting turned communal.

And then came levitation.

Witnesses—including Ed and Lorraine Warren themselves—attested to the impossible. During a séance, Carolyn was lifted chest-high from a chair, hovering without support. Her face was rigid, her eyes black with unnatural intensity, as though controlled by another entity. She spoke languages unknown to her—words that twisted in the air and died on her lips. Overwhelmed, she crashed back to the floor, breaking the chair beneath her. Ed, shocked by the raw display, reportedly knelt beside her trembling body.

Similar levitation events were reported by house guests. One visitor—a Warren associate—saw a bedroom light explode without any wiring fault, unusually bright, before dimming to reveal that nothing remained but a scorched bulb nestling in blackened ceiling plaster.

By 1975, house guests experienced harrowing impressions: they awoke in the middle of the night to feel unseen presences leaning over them, pulling blanket off, pushing at their bodies. Some reported bruises on their arms, bruises that resembled three-pronged claw marks. They awoke in the morning smelling the same foul stench that had tormented Carolyn. Perhaps most disturbing, furniture used regularly would later be found placed in spaces where it could easily harm someone stepping in—a chair facing the sharp corner of a table, for instance.

The Warrens documented patterns of "oppression" and "possession" throughout 1974–75. Lorraine, the clairvoyant, described an increasing resistance whenever they tried to pray or bless the house—an unseen force pushing petitions away, like a windstorm over the candlelight.

Even Roger, the final skeptic, had an experience. One evening, after telling the visiting Warrens to leave, he refused. Moments later, he awoke to find his clothes folded neatly at the foot of his bed—down to his socks. With dawn, he discovered marks on the wooden floor where he had slept: long, deeply gouged grooves resembling the underside of a wooden beam dragged across the floor. He never denied the haunting again.

In the space of months, what began as whispers had grown into paralyzing aggression. The Perron home was no longer merely haunted—it was possessed, its occupants under siege. The spirits—especially Bathsheba—no longer hovered on the threshold. They pushed through it.

SECTION III:
DOCUMENTING
THE NIGHTMARE

Chapter 9: Seeking Help

By the spring of 1974, the Perron home had turned from sanctuary to battleground. What had started as unsettling whispers and bruises on Carolyn had escalated to aggressive hauntings that threatened the safety and unity of the family. With events growing unmanageable, the Perrons launched a desperate attempt to find help beyond their walls.

Their first outreach was to a local Catholic priest, Father Ralph Fadden of St. Theresa Parish. Carolyn had grown up in the church and believed spiritual guidance might calm the storm. She arranged a meeting: the priest would come, pray, and bless the house—a traditional foundation for peace. For two days, Father Fadden led prayers in each room. He sprinkled holy water along doorframes and around bedrooms. But three days later, Carolyn awoke with bruises on her arms; the oppressive odor was stronger and longer-lasting than ever before. When she called for help, the answer came gently but firmly: Father Fadden suggested, "This might require more... specialized assistance." The words were cordial, but their implication— that only exorcism-level intervention could help—terrified Carolyn more than any bruise or odor.

Next, Roger called the local authorities. In 1971, Harrisville had no police department; the town relied on the Rhode Island State Police, stationed some miles away. Roger lodged a report of "suspicious activity": doors opening, inexplicable noises, the family dog snarling at the basement. But the officers who came were skeptical. They found no signs of forced entry, no burglars, nothing physical. "You've got an old house," they told him kindly. "It needs repairs, not prayers." Roger's hopes faltered. Rather than filing a criminal case, the police gently suggested he seek local mental health services, worrying the family might be unstable.

Word of "ghost hysteria" spread. Neighbors exchanged sympathetic smiles, but kept their distance. An aunt, visiting for afternoon tea, left after a single evening, citing overwork and the "tension in the air." The children noticed. Nancy, Christine, Cindy, April— they all heard other aunts say, "Maybe she's just stressed." The fear of being labeled delusional or mentally unwell began to scare the family more than the unexplained bruises and smells.

The Warrens were the next lifeline. Ed and Lorraine were recommended by another priest who said they "understood things beyond the physical." They arrived in October 1973 and spent weeks documenting the phenomenon. Their team recorded EVP sessions ("Are you a friend?"), collected audio tapes and placed bells and cameras to capture movement. Their notes described "oppressive hits and pushes" on Carolyn, "aching bruises," and at one point, the door being locked from the inside when no one was present. When Lorraine sensed Bathsheba's presence, she claimed it had "a long neck and an old face, angry and uneven."

Local media had yet to arrive, and town authorities were only drawn in after a particularly violent event. Roger came downstairs one morning to find a "witch's mark" on the wall—a charred-looking symbol etched into wood beside the foyer. Intrigued, a Rhode Island State Police investigator returned, took photos, and ruled out accelerant or fire damage. The police report ended with a cryptic line: "No physical perpetrator identified; unexplained phenomenon."

By late 1973, the Perrons found themselves caught between worlds: the church of everyday miracles that didn't suffice, skepticism from civic institutions, and the Warrens' spiritual approach, which was controversial yet hopeful. They were tired, afraid, and increasingly isolated. What had begun as a dream of land and family life had become a gauntlet of disbelief and haunting. Yet, they persisted, clinging to each other and to the tiny hope that someone—anyone—would finally understand.

Chapter 10: Enter the Warrens

The air was already heavy when they arrived.

October had settled into the Rhode Island countryside with a strange stillness that year, and the trees near Round Top Road rustled without wind. The Perrons stood on the porch of the old farmhouse, their eyes hollow from too many sleepless nights. They watched the dark sedan roll up the gravel path and stop with a soft sigh of dust. Out stepped a couple who, though unknown to them in person, already felt like their last hope.

Ed and Lorraine Warren.

Ed, dressed in a dark overcoat with a thin folder tucked under one arm, took a slow look around the property as if he were reading it. Lorraine, serene and pale, kept her gaze fixed on the house. Her eyes didn't scan the architecture or the woods behind—it was as though she was seeing something else entirely. Carolyn Perron knew then that this woman was different.

Inside, the warmth of the kitchen did little to dispel the cold that clung to the rest of the house. Roger offered coffee, which Lorraine politely declined. "Thank you," she said softly, "but I think it's best I go room by room before anything changes."

Carolyn led her upstairs first. Lorraine didn't speak; she just walked slowly, her fingers brushing the walls. Sometimes she'd stop and close her eyes. Once, in the girls' bedroom, she paused near the window and whispered, "Pain... here. A woman cries at night, but not for her children."

Downstairs, Ed took notes while speaking with the Perrons one by one. Andrea, oldest of the five daughters, had her journal open already, filled with shaky handwriting and rough sketches of faces no one recognized. Nancy and Christine described waking up at night to whispers in their ears. April mentioned Manny, the boy who played hide-and-seek and never lost. And Carolyn… she sat last. Her voice shook as she told them about the bruises, the smells, the unseen hands that gripped her chest in the night.

They listened. They didn't question her sanity, didn't offer platitudes or call it imagination. Ed simply nodded and wrote it all down.

In the days that followed, the Warrens began their investigation. They brought in tools: tape recorders, motion-sensitive bells, crucifixes, and cameras. Lorraine walked the house in silence, sometimes humming, sometimes holding her cross tightly to her chest. In the parlor, she said she could see shadows move even when the room stood still. In the cellar, she refused to go alone. "There's something older down here," she told Ed, "and it doesn't want us speaking its name."

The children, curious but cautious, began to watch the investigators with quiet reverence. For the first time, someone was treating what they were experiencing as real.

Then came the séance.

It was a bitter night. Wind clawed at the windows, though the forecast had called for calm skies. The Warrens set up in the old dining room. Lorraine sat in a wooden chair at the center of the circle, Carolyn to her right, Ed opposite, and Andrea crouched quietly in a corner behind a sideboard, scribbling everything she saw.

They began with prayer. The room dimmed, not from light, but from weight. It felt like the air itself was sinking. As Lorraine reached out to Carolyn and the others, her voice took on a rhythm—steady, firm, gentle. The prayer shifted to invocation. And then, suddenly, Carolyn jerked back in her chair.

Her body stiffened. Her hands gripped the sides. Her head tilted slowly to the right, then snapped forward. A guttural voice—one no one recognized—spoke words they couldn't understand. The lights flickered. One of the bells tied to a beam rang violently, even though no one had touched it.

Roger rushed forward to grab his wife, but Ed blocked him. "Don't touch her," he ordered. "You'll only make it worse."

Carolyn's face twisted—not in pain, but in rage. She screamed a name—Bathsheba—and then crumpled. The room fell silent, save for her sobs and Lorraine's low chant as she tried to draw whatever presence had invaded back out.

When it was over, Carolyn lay limp on the floor. Andrea never forgot how her mother looked that night: smaller, somehow, as if part of her had been carved away. Roger carried her to bed while Lorraine sat alone in the darkened dining room, eyes closed, lips moving soundlessly.

In the aftermath, Ed declared that what they were dealing with was no ordinary ghost. "This is oppression," he said. "This is something demonic."

But the Church would not approve an exorcism—not yet. And so, the Warrens returned week after week, documenting, praying, and doing what they could. They asked the family to remain calm, to hold tight to faith. But even they could sense that something had been disturbed during the séance—something that would not retreat easily.

For the Perrons, the arrival of the Warrens had been a lifeline.

For the house, it had been a challenge.

Chapter 11: Interviews and Examinations

After the intensity of the séance, a sense of purpose settled over the house. The Warrens were no longer visitors—they were investigators, gathering every detail, every shadow, every whisper to understand what lived within these walls.

Early one morning in November, Ed sat at the kitchen table with Roger and Carolyn before dawn's light filled the room. He opened his notebook and began asking questions in a calm, methodical way. Roger described the tremors he felt in the morning, the inexplicable cold spots in hallways, and the increasing luminous haze that hovered at the top of the staircase. He noted the times, places, and nature of each event. Roger answered without shame—he had decided to trust rather than dismiss.

Meanwhile, Lorraine began exploring the upstairs bedrooms. She chatted gently with Andrea and her sisters, encouraging them to speak freely. Andrea recited passages from her journals—dreams, night visions, and moments when lights had faded or whispers had drawn her into the hall. Nancy and Christine spoke of hearing their names at odd hours; Cindy described how she and April sometimes saw a man drifting aimlessly just out of focus. Lorraine listened without judgment, but her pen moved swiftly—each subplot a thread in the growing tapestry of evidence.

By the week's end, the Warrens had set up an operational base. Tape recorders and EVP units dotted shelves, and bells layered like tripwires across hallways. Lorraine asked Andrea to read aloud in each room— Bible verses, prayers, and simple statements—while a recorder picked up every nuance. On playback, they heard faint responses—stray syllables, odd resonance, or sudden silences that swallowed her voice as if something was listening.

A small infrared camera was placed at the top of the basement stairs. Overnight, when no one was present, it captured a soft blue light glowing where the walls met the floor—a motionless haze that ebbed like breath and disappeared by dawn. The Warrens examined the tapes and stills with meticulous focus, pausing frame by frame to study shapes hidden within darkness.

Lorraine's readings continued. Some sessions were scheduled at set intervals—with Carolyn seated in the center, Lorraine on one side, and the room filled with the sisters, each holding a candle. During these, Lorraine sometimes murmured in an altered voice, relaying impressions: a woman wearing black, a forced weight pressing on a heart, a presence trying to force its way into speech. Afterwards, she'd transcribe the session word for word, mark the time stamps of greatest intensity, and draw diagrams showing energy pooling in corners.

Ed tracked physical changes in the house. Thermometers seemed to dip five degrees at random and cluster around the basement hours. Walls showed strange new cracks that formed in no detectable pattern. A chair leg swung as though tethered—visible on tape—that rock solidly moved forward before snapping back while no one was near. He collected fragments: a broken rosary from the master bedroom, a handful of rose petals scattered in the kitchen— though no one saw them appear.

A medical doctor who visited for unrelated reasons examined Carolyn's bruises. They were not consistent with accidents or typical blood disorders. Ed noted that similar marks were emerging on Andrea and Nancy—small abrasions shaping into distinct triangular patterns, not scratches or bites, but embedded like impressions of claws.

This was no longer anecdotal; it was a file. A body of evidence. The Warrens would later claim that across eighty interviews, dozens of recordings, and multiple sessions, they documented patterns—voices that answered questions, lights that responded to prayer, receding cold zones as blessings progressed. Their records show timestamps, room coordinates, and object placement logs that built a precise chronology.

They were not just storytellers—they were gathering data, building a case. When asked years later why they did this work, Lorraine said it was "to give voices to those who could not speak, and to give proof to those who would not believe."

By the time 1974 ended, the Warrens had amassed hours of audio, stacks of detailed notes, and rooms of photographic evidence. Interviews with attendees—neighbors, a visiting pastor—added layers of third-party testimony: the pastor had heard chanting in the basement; the aunt had smelled the same foul stench during a brief afternoon visit.

The result was a dossier—thick, textured, precise—that reframed the Perron home from a setting of fear to a site of investigation. And in that shift—evidence over emotion—the Perron case moved toward the public eye. What was once whispers in the night became data on a page. And that evidence would soon face scrutiny on a very public stage.

Chapter 12: A Night of Terror (The Séance)

The farmhouse had fallen into a strange kind of silence. Not the peaceful kind that comes with dusk settling on the woods, but a pressure-filled stillness—like the moment before a storm cracks open the sky. Everyone in the Perron household felt it. The tension between the walls. The hum in the floorboards. Something was waiting.

It had been weeks since the Warrens first arrived. Their investigations had filled the house with equipment and prayer, holy water and hushed interviews. But the unease persisted, growing sharper. Ed knew it. Lorraine knew it. And Carolyn—most of all—could feel it gnawing at her skin. That was when the decision was made: they would hold a séance.

The night chosen was cold and damp, the kind of night that clung to the skin. Rain whispered on the windows, barely audible. The lights were dimmed, the candles arranged in a circle on the old wooden dining room table. Lorraine sat at the head, her rosary coiled tightly around her hand. Ed stood beside her, ever the anchor. Carolyn took her place across from them, hands trembling slightly as she rested them on the tabletop. The other participants—friends, a local priest, Andrea, and two of her sisters—formed the circle in silence.

Lorraine began with prayer, her voice barely rising above a whisper. A Latin chant followed. The air thickened. It was as if the walls themselves leaned in to listen.

Carolyn's eyes closed.

At first, nothing happened. Only the flames danced. The house breathed.

Then Carolyn began to shift. Her breathing deepened. Her shoulders hunched as if an invisible weight pressed against them. And then—her head snapped back. A guttural sound erupted from her throat, not quite a scream, but not human either. A harsh, warping growl that silenced the room.

Her body stiffened. The chair beneath her legs began to creak—slowly, impossibly—rising. It lifted off the ground, just inches at first, then more. The room gasped. Andrea gripped the table, watching in horror as her mother's body floated above the floor, arms stiff, hands clawed.

Carolyn's mouth moved. Words spilled out, but none that anyone could understand. They were broken syllables, sharp and wet, spoken in a voice that didn't belong to her. Lorraine's face went pale. Ed began reciting a binding prayer, voice loud, commanding. The priest beside him followed suit, voice shaking.

Then, without warning, the chair shot backward.

Carolyn was thrown like a rag doll across the room, landing hard against the floor. The candles extinguished in a sudden gust. For a moment, it was pitch black.

Screams. Shouts. Chaos.

Someone turned on a lamp. Andrea scrambled toward her mother, who lay crumpled on the floor, eyes fluttering, lips trembling. Lorraine dropped to her knees beside her, whispering prayers under her breath.

When Carolyn opened her eyes, she looked blank—lost. She didn't remember what had happened. Not the chair, not the voice, not the levitation. All she knew was pain in her ribs and a hollow ache in her chest.

The séance had ended, but whatever had been stirred up hadn't gone quietly.

The following day, Carolyn could barely stand. Roger carried her to a nearby clinic where bruises were found on her back and legs—deep, purple, and inexplicable. The doctor noted she seemed "drained of energy," but found no internal injuries. No one spoke of what had happened inside the farmhouse. No one would believe it anyway.

Andrea stayed silent most of the day, but in the evening, she sat with her mother in the dim living room and asked quietly, "Do you think it was her?"

Carolyn didn't answer right away.

"I don't know," she whispered. "But something... something wants us gone."

From that night onward, things changed.

The house no longer simply disturbed them—it watched them. Every corner seemed darker, every creak of the stairs more pronounced. Carolyn stopped sleeping in the master bedroom. The children avoided the cellar altogether. Lorraine, deeply shaken by what she had seen, warned that what they'd encountered wasn't just a spirit—it was something older, something angry.

The Warrens didn't attempt another séance. They brought in more holy objects, recited stronger prayers, but something had shifted. The house had revealed its hand.

Ed wanted to request a formal exorcism from the Church. But Roger, terrified and humiliated, refused. He had seen enough. He wanted them out. He didn't want more priests, more attention, more darkness drawn into their lives.

The Warrens respected his wishes and scaled back their visits, but they remained in contact, advising the Perrons through letters and phone calls. Andrea kept journaling. The recordings were stored. And Carolyn never again spoke of that night in detail.

But Andrea remembered it all. She would carry the memory for decades. The way the room felt like it collapsed in on itself. The sound her mother made as she rose off the floor. The look in her eyes when it was all over—like someone who had gone somewhere else and barely made it back.

It was not just a haunting anymore.

It was war.

Chapter 13: Aftermath and Fallout

The morning after the séance felt hollow. The candles had burned to stubs; the furniture lay askew. The air no longer smelled of must or candle smoke but of something washed away—yet still lingering, like a memory. In that silence, the Perron family exhaled, collectively and warily.

Carolyn lay in bed, bruised, exhausted, her spirit battered from the ordeal. The clinic report confirmed what the Perrons already knew: her ribcage marked with vivid bruises, her movements tentative, her eyes haunted by ineffable pain. But there was no fracture, no disease—only the signs of something otherworldly.

In the days that followed, the Warrens compiled their final report—a dossier spanning 80 interviews, audio and video logs, EVP transcriptions, and photographic proof of drifting lights or unmoved furniture. They wrote matter-of-factly that the house was "spirit-saturated" and that Carolyn had been physically manifesting oppression in the form of bruises, smells, and levitations. They ultimately concluded the haunting was demonic in nature, centered on the presence of a negative entity they believed to be Bathsheba Sherman.

But the Perrons were left dealing with something else—trauma colder than any ghost.

Andrea Perron, then in her early teens, stopped sleeping. She would lie awake, listening for echoes in the walls, waiting for a figure to appear at her door. Cindy and Christine clung to their mother, insisting on shared rooms. Nancy refused to touch the piano she once loved; its keys felt like a portal. April, the youngest, sometimes froze mid-sentence in the kitchen, her face drained of color for reasons none could explain.

For Roger, the ordeal was a crucible. He watched the strength of the man who once dismissed ghosts collapse under the weight of fear and regret. He spent nights pacing the driveway, hands buried in pockets, questioning whether he'd brought his family here. He had seen the evidence—so had the Warrens—but still, that late-night solitude told him something deeper had changed inside this house—and inside himself.

But there was a stubbornness wedged into their survival. They couldn't leave—not yet. Financial realities bound them; selling a home believed to be haunted didn't happen overnight. More than that, Carolyn had grown anchored to the place in an unearthly way. She admitted, finally: "I cannot leave. It knows me."

So they stayed—and fought back. With the Warrens' blessing, they stayed year after year. Ed prescribed daily prayers; Lorraine gifted them holy water, salt, and prayers written on stiff yellow paper. They set boundaries at doorways and protected each of the daughters at bedtime. Over time, the Bruises faded; the odors lessened; the lights flickered, but less often. The house's presence became quieter, though not entirely gone.

The Warrens visited only sporadically after 1975, but they never fully severed ties. Ed said later the Perron home was one of the most intense cases he ever saw—and that it stayed in his mind until his death. He never secured Vatican approval for an exorcism, as the priest advised, but he held few illusions: the entity was ancient and powerful. Even Lorraine stated that what they'd experienced wasn't a haunting—they had witnessed a spiritual crisis that required vigilance, not escape.

As years passed, the family rebuilt some normalcy. The children returned to school, pets were rehomed, curtains opened. But there was always hesitation: the middle hallway remained off-limits at night. The girls refused to stay alone. Carolyn changed her prayer habits—more prayer, less sleep. Roger joined in, kneeling at the kitchen table each evening.

In 1980, they left—the farmhouse sold—but they carried the house inside them. Some neighbors later said the haunting eased after they moved. Others whispered of visitors who left screaming during renovations. The new owners, Michael and Norma

Sutcliffe, claimed modest remnants—chairs shifting, whispers late at night—but nothing compared to the Perrons' decade of terror.

Andrea would later reflect: the haunting never truly ended when they moved. It ended when they chose peace. They could leave the land behind, but not the echoes it had imprinted on their souls.

Why the Perrons Stayed

1.**Financial Entanglement** – A traditional mortgage, low resale interest, fear of eviction costs.

2.**Spiritual Attachment** – Carolyn's conviction that you couldn't simply walk away.

3.**Protective Vow** – The family stayed as guardians of what had been unleashed.

4.**Faith as Armor** – Their identity reshaped to include resistance and resilience.

Warrens' Final Conclusion

The Perron haunting became, in Ed's mind, a case study—proof that evil could live in ordinary walls, but that faith, vigilance, and trust could contain it.

Lorraine's final notes express no triumph, only resolution:

"The family survived. We stayed. The house remains, odd in its quiet. Will Bathsheba or old survivors ever return? Possibly. But so long as this family prays, so long as they guard this threshold, they are not victim. They are witness."

SECTION IV:
FACTS, FILES &
FALSITIES

Chapter 14: Truth vs. Legend

For decades, whispers echoed louder than records in the woods of Harrisville. Among the tangle of roots and cellar stones, stories grew—stories of witches, of rituals, of deaths that stained the land. At the heart of those whispers stood one name: Bathsheba Sherman.

To the Perron family, the name was not folklore. It was force. They believed she haunted their home— watched them, tormented them, clung to the walls like ivy wrapping an old house. Andrea Perron spoke of her with certainty, even reverence. After all, her mother had been choked, tossed, and bruised in a séance where the name Bathsheba had first emerged. But where did this story begin?

To answer that, one must step back into time—not into a spirit realm, but into town halls and dusty archives.

Bathsheba Thayer was born in 1812, long before the Perrons ever set foot in Rhode Island. She married a man named Judson Sherman, and together they lived on a nearby farm—not the Arnold Estate. Their land was peaceful, surrounded by orchards and woods. By every known account, Bathsheba was a farmer's wife and a mother. She had four children, though only one survived into adulthood. The others died young— tragic, but not unusual for the time. The records list their causes of death as childhood illnesses. There were no charges. No trials. No accusations of murder.

Still, legend claimed otherwise.

People began to say that Bathsheba sacrificed an infant to Satan, that she was caught in the act, and hung herself in shame from a tree in the backyard of the Arnold Estate. But there's no record of any such death. Bathsheba died in 1885 of a stroke—called "paralysis" in her death notice—and was buried beside her husband in a quiet cemetery just a few miles away. Her stone still stands, weatherworn and often vandalized by thrill-seekers convinced they're standing above a witch.

So, how did her name become poison?

Some believe it started with a misinterpretation—perhaps a psychic impression from Lorraine Warren or a whispered suspicion passed between neighbors. Others suggest the story needed a villain. When you live in a house filled with shadows and voices, it's easier to fight something with a name. Bathsheba became the face of the unknown.

But the tragedy didn't stop with her.

The so-called "Black Book of Burrillville" tells of suicides, drownings, poisonings—family after family cursed by the land. It's true that over the centuries, people died in and around the farmhouse. But in the cold light of documents and gravestones, most of these deaths lose their sinister edge.

Susan Arnold did hang herself, but in a different home. Prudence Arnold was indeed murdered, but that happened in Massachusetts, not Harrisville. Jarvis Smith, a drifter, froze to death near the property—but his connection to the land was brief, and his death was natural. Other tragedies—children lost to typhus, men who never came home from war—were all real. But they were not ghosts. They were history.

Yet, the myths endure.

Why? Because they serve a purpose.

The myth of Bathsheba gives structure to the terror. It explains what can't be explained. It lets people point to a grave and say, "There. That's where it started." It gives the house its villain, its dark queen.

But perhaps the truth is more complex than any one spirit. Perhaps the land carries a weight—not just of one woman, but of centuries of lives lived hard and lost early. The walls of the farmhouse have heard laughter, screams, lullabies, and arguments. They remember. And memory, too, can haunt.

For every thrill-seeker who comes to the house looking for Bathsheba's curse, there are town historians who sigh. They see her as a misunderstood widow—a woman whose tragedy was twisted by rumor into horror.

Maybe Bathsheba was never the villain. Maybe she, too, is a victim of grief, of time, and of a story that ran wild in the dark.

Chapter 15: Scientific or Supernatural?

Years after the Perrons left the farmhouse behind, the house remained quiet. No more séances. No more screaming children. Just dust, silence, and memory. But while the rooms no longer echoed with voices, the world outside buzzed with theories.

Scientists, psychologists, skeptics—they all came, not to drive out spirits, but to explain them.

In a quiet office, hundreds of miles away, a sleep researcher watched footage of Carolyn Perron describing the nights she awoke unable to move. Her eyes had told the story long before her words did. "Something was sitting on my chest," she had said. "I could feel its breath." To her, it was an evil force. But to the man in the lab coat, it was a textbook case of sleep paralysis.

He'd seen it many times. A brain trapped between dreaming and waking, the body still paralyzed by REM sleep. Hallucinations would rush in—shadowy figures at the foot of the bed, whispers just behind the ears, a crushing weight. It was terrifying. And real. But not supernatural.

In that moment, Carolyn's haunting didn't seem so far from science.

Meanwhile, in another part of the country, an acoustic engineer named Lydia stepped into the old farmhouse with a frequency meter. She wasn't looking for ghosts. She was listening for vibrations. The kind humans can't hear—but can feel. Infrasound.

In the dining room, she paused.

"This," she whispered, "feels like a pressure behind the eyes. Makes you anxious. Makes your skin crawl." The windows were shut. No wind. No wires humming. But still, the feeling persisted.

Lydia had studied the effects of low-frequency sound waves. She knew they could cause nausea, unease, even full-blown hallucinations if the conditions were right. Could the house's old wooden beams, its long-forgotten plumbing, be creating sounds that stirred the imagination? Or worse—mimicked terror?

She jotted a note and moved on, but a thought clung to her: perhaps the house didn't need ghosts. Perhaps it was the ghost.

Back in town, a psychologist reviewed the Perron case and shook his head, not in disbelief, but in recognition. Five children, each entering or passing through adolescence. Emotional stress. Constant fear. Suggestibility. It was a formula he'd seen before in poltergeist cases—especially those involving families.

He remembered Andrea's stories of books flying, doors slamming, and toys moving on their own. In the psychologist's mind, it didn't point to spirits, but to stress made manifest. "When the brain can't express emotion," he explained, "the body sometimes does it for you. And in the right environment, the group begins to feed off each other."

He didn't accuse the Perrons of lying. Quite the opposite—he believed they were telling the truth, as they experienced it. But their truth, he thought, might be a psychological phenomenon wrapped in fear, grief, and belief.

Still, none of these people—neither the sleep researcher, nor the sound engineer, nor the psychologist—could explain everything.

- Levitation?
- Bruises?
- Voices calling names in the dark?

Each one had a theory. But none had certainty. And that's where the story deepened.

Even the skeptics, sitting at their desks, had to admit: something happened in that house. Something powerful. Something transformative. Maybe it was science. Maybe something else entirely. Maybe both.

Andrea once said, "You don't walk out of that house the same person who walked in." And perhaps that was the answer.

The haunting had layers—psychological, emotional, and environmental. There were no ghosts to catch, no demons to confront. But there was fear. And fear, if nurtured, becomes shape. It becomes present.

In the end, what the Perrons experienced might never be proven one way or the other. Scientists could point to data. Paranormal researchers could point to their recordings. The truth, like the house itself, sat in between.

Not completely explainable.

Not completely unimaginable.

A haunting, perhaps, of both the mind and the world around it.

Chapter 16: Investigators Weigh In

Long after the Perrons had fled the Arnold Estate, and long after the Warrens had packed away their holy water and cassette tapes, the house remained. Silent. Still. Waiting.

But it was far from forgotten.

The old farmhouse began to attract a new breed of visitor—men and women who came not with prayers or exorcisms, but with meters, thermometers, voice recorders, and skepticism. Some believed they were hunting proof. Others believed they were hunting delusion. What they all shared was one question: What really happened in Harrisville?

The Skeptic in the Shadows

It was a rainy spring morning when a writer, an investigator more comfortable in libraries than in seance circles, pulled into the driveway of the Arnold Estate. The new owners, a quiet couple who had long grown weary of being associated with Hollywood horror, welcomed him hesitantly.

He walked the rooms slowly. In the cellar, he knelt by the furnace and touched the crumbling walls. Upstairs, he listened to the creaks and groans of aging wood. No ghosts. Just drafty rooms, faulty latches, and the wind.

"Most of this," he muttered into his recorder, "can be explained."

But even as he dismissed the stories as misunderstood noise and the natural decay of an old structure, he paused on the staircase—where Carolyn had once claimed to see a dark figure—and felt a chill that made him second-guess, if only for a moment.

Voices in the Static

Then came the investigators with blinking boxes and antennae. Paranormal teams—some with YouTube channels, others with private journals—descended on the farmhouse.

They brought EVP recorders, hoping to catch the voices of the dead. And sometimes, they did. A faint "hello," a whisper of a child's laughter, or a breathless phrase like "get out" would rise from the static.

To believers, these were not coincidences. They were confirmations.

One night, a group huddled in the basement, asked, "Is anyone here with us?" The silence seemed to stretch unnaturally long. Then, a quiet voice on playback: "Mommy…"

But skeptics countered with simpler explanations—radio interference, wind through the cracks, even the subconscious mind filling in sounds that weren't truly there.

Ghosts in the Thermals

Others brought infrared cameras. They swept through the house, filming in green-tinted night vision. In the parlor, a cold spot hovered near the fireplace—

unmoving, colder than the surrounding room. Was it a spirit? A draft? A difference in insulation?

In one recording, a human-shaped silhouette appeared briefly, standing just behind a doorway. It didn't move. It didn't speak. And when they ran into the room—it was gone.

To the crew, it was the proof they'd come for.

To skeptics, it was just another trick of light and shadows, exaggerated by the grainy lens of infrared.

Flickering Between Worlds

They came one by one—filmmakers, psychics, engineers, paranormal teams, authors, skeptics. Some left with wide eyes and trembling hands, convinced they had encountered the beyond. Others left with notebooks and data logs, unmoved, certain they had seen only the mechanics of an old house playing tricks.

What emerged from these visits was not resolution, but reflection.

Because the house had changed.

Not physically. But spiritually. Culturally. Emotionally.

It had become a mirror.

What you believed when you entered determined what you saw when you left.

The Evidence That Wasn't

No official documentation ever proved the house was haunted. There were no conclusive photographs, no universally accepted recordings, no government files or scientific validation.

But there were notebooks. Diaries. Audio files filled with static and whispers. Photos with shadows that didn't belong. And personal testimonies—many deeply emotional, some even life-changing.

In the world of the paranormal, that was enough.

In the world of science, it wasn't.

The House Today

Even now, the Arnold Estate sits quietly among the trees of Harrisville. Paranormal tours come and go. Cameras still roll in the darkness. And sometimes, if you listen closely, someone swears they heard a voice that wasn't there. ·

What the investigators found—paranormal or not—
was this: the house remembers.

And it doesn't care who believes it.

Chapter 17: The Perrons Speak Out

Decades after that chilling winter at the Arnold Estate, the Perron family found their voices once again—not in whispers across cold hallways, but in published pages, interviews, and documentaries. Their story had aged like reputation—it grew richer, more nuanced, and far more public.

Andrea's Memoir: A Daughter's Truth

It was in 2011 when Andrea Perron, the eldest daughter who once scribbled tremulous notes by candlelight, released her memoir House of Darkness, House of Light. The book spilled onto the page with vivid clarity—more than terror and trauma, there was humanity, wonder, and unfiltered insight into childhood under siege.

Andrea described séances lit with hope rather than horror. She wrote of spirits she called "benevolent" and "cordial," not just malevolent forces. Among these was a spirit she never named, but who she said "taught me compassion, rather than fear."

The memoir became part of the Perrons' living testament. It framed their presence at the house not rooted in sensationalism, but in sincerity.

A Voice in Documentaries

The next decade brought cameras and crowds. In 2021, Andrea sat down for Bathsheba: Search for Evil, a documentary filmed with calm reflection rather than jump cuts. She described her family's choice to reclaim their story:

"The producers read my books, and nothing was exaggerated. What the Warrens recorded is only the beginning," she said.

"It wasn't Bathsheba who tormented my mother—it was someone else entirely."

Andrea clarified that Bathsheba Sherman's legend—a witch with a broken neck—was not her family's spirit.

She told viewers that the spirit was likely Mrs. Arnold, a woman who died by suicide in the barn centuries earlier.

When asked whether the haunting could have been a blessing, she nodded firmly. Witnessing a realm beyond death, she said, offered "a faith not frightened by the dark."

A Sister Speaks

Her younger sisters joined too. In speaking tours and live events, Nancy and Christine stood beside Andrea and Roger. They told modern audiences about pneumonic choking, midnight bruises, and the resilience forged in cold rooms.

In a livestream at the old house, they guided viewers through the hallway where clocks stopped—and recited passages for protection. April, the youngest, now gone after an accidental overdose, featured in their memories as a child whose spirit still ran through those halls.

Critiquing "The Conjuring" Myth

When James Wan's The Conjuring franchise hit screens in 2013, it was terrifying—but only 5% aligned with the Perrons' reality, Andrea later said. The filmmakers invented a Bathsheba witch with malevolent intent to enhance the mythos.

Andrea reframed the story: the farmhouse was a "portal cleverly disguised as a farmhouse"—not a cage. It was home, for better and worse.

Living with the Legacy

Today, the farmhouse—now a tourism site—draws visitors and investigators. Andrea returns, she says, not as a haunted child, but as a guardian and guide. She walks the halls with purpose. She knows every stair crease, every cold draft, every story embedded in the wood.

She has no fear of death, she tells audiences, because she has known something beyond it.

A Family's Journey

The Perrons have come far from the shadows to the spotlight. Their story evolved from whispered fears into public testimony, not for fame, but for understanding.

What began as a survival story became a spiritual journey. From trembling daughters to authors and speakers, they turned trauma into testimony. Whether audiences believe in ghosts or not, they cannot deny the power of that.

SECTION V:
HOLLYWOOD &
THE HAUNTING

Chapter 18: A Haunting Goes Hollywood

In the spring of 2010, the Perrons received an unusual call—one that felt both surreal and inevitable. Hollywood had come knocking on their old farmhouse. James Wan, the rising director of chilling, atmospheric horror, and Warner Bros., had decided to bring the Perrons' true story to the silver screen.

From Case File to Screenplay

In dimly lit production offices, James Wan and the Hayeses poured over Ed and Lorraine Warren's case files, recordings, and notes. Lorraine became a consultant, offering emotional guidance and ensuring that certain key scenes remained intact, while the studio insisted on adding cinematic flourishes. Wan recalled being told the film needed to feel like reality… but still keep audiences glued to their seats.

In Wilmington, North Carolina, sets were built to mimic the farmhouse, down to the dusty yellow clock that stopped at 3:07 a.m. Junior members of the Perron clan quietly visited the set, less to supervise than to preserve their memories of fear and home.

Real Meets Fiction

In early screenings, audiences gasped. The Conjuring opened with a séance that mirrored family lore— Carolyn levitated, rattling bells, whispering. But the movie introduced extras: a secret basement room of horrors, multiple family tragedies, flesh-eating demonic cops. The filmmakers admitted freely that 95% was fictional. The real haunting had occurred over a decade; in the film, it unfolded in a single night.

Still, the filmmakers kept the emotional core. Andrea, watching a screening, later told a reporter that the familial warmth and the crushing dread were both real. She said the filmmakers "went to bat for the truth" even while embellishing details for effect.

When Audience Meets Myth

The Conjuring premiered in July 2013. It shattered horror stereotypes—not for shock or gore, but for emotional weight. It grossed over $320□million worldwide, marking a milestone in modern horror. Critics praised its restraint; audiences hailed every flicker in the dark. The film became a phenomenon, spawning a now-billion-dollar "Conjuring Universe".

For the Perrons, it meant something else entirely. The house, once hidden by woods, now sat under a glare of attention. Ghost tourism soared. Fans wanted photos of "Bathsheba's window"; YouTubers raced to capture shadows in hallways.

Myths Recast and Corrections Issued

Shortly after the film, Andrea spoke up, both in interviews and documentaries: Bathsheba Sherman was not a witch, did not live in their house, and never sacrificed a baby. Lorraine had simply referred to a dark presence as "Bathsheba," and that name stuck in the narrative echo chamber.

Andrea explained that the true spirit they encountered was "more sorrowful than evil"—an Arkene Arnold, who'd lost her child and died tragically. She praised the movie for capturing emotional truth, but warned audiences against reading it as literal history.

Hollywood's Ripple Effect

The film's success created a surge in interest. Eau de Bathsheba merchandise appeared. The farmhouse was sold, and new owners opened it to ghost hunts, charging upwards of $1,500 a night.

Paranormal investigators—the new wave—fanned out into the field with EVP recorders and infrared cameras. Meanwhile, historians and skeptics rushed to set the record straight, researching land records and birth certificates to debunk myths.

Audiences stood divided: some found solace in the family's survival. Others revelled in cinematic suspense, embracing the myth. Everywhere, the house stood unchanged, but bathed in new meaning.

A Legacy Beyond Fear

Today, when James Wan speaks, he refers to the Perrons not as source material, but as partners in giving weight to fear. Andrea, Nancy, and Christine regularly appear on panels, talk shows, and podcasts—not to relive trauma, but to own it.

The farmhouse still stands, but the haunting lives in memory, media, and moral questions. Did Hollywood bring justice to their story? Did it warp their truth?

In that gray zone between reality and legend, the Perron family remains the final authority—keepers of a haunting that, Hollywood or not, forever taught us how love stands between fear and faith.

Chapter 19: Paranormal Tourism

The old yellow colonial house once belonging to the Perrons stood as before—roof weathered, shutters faded, silence echoing through empty halls. But the silence never lasted long. Once the story hit the big screen, interest surged, transforming the house into a magnet for those drawn to the supernatural.

The Reopening

It began in 2019, when Cory and Jennifer Heinzen— paranormal enthusiasts from Maine—bought the property. With respect and curiosity, they curated "day tours" and small evening investigations. Visitors first strolled through the familiar living room, eyes widening at the yellow clock rumored to stop at 3:07□a.m. Then, in hushed breathing, they'd hear about candle flickers, soft knocks, and house chills—

the faint echoes of what once tore the Perron family apart.

By 2022, the property changed hands again. Jacqueline Núñez, a self-described medium, purchased it with grand plans: overnight stays, guided "ghost hunts," and even camping sites—dubbed "ghamping"—for the adventurous. Tents were pitched around the barn, and by night, portable fire pits flickered while participants shared stories of drumming from the 1675 battlefields nearby or distant, childlike footsteps.

Ghost Hunters, YouTubers, Skeptics—Oh My

Soon, curiosity escalated into a full-blown spectacle. YouTube personalities with cameras in hand arrived to record each creak. Fans captured fuzzy silhouettes on infrared and claimed voices caught on EVP: soft murmurs asking, "Mommy?" Paranormal teams armed with EMF meters and night vision prowled the hallways, hoping to recreate the Perrons' nights of terror.

In 2022, Sam & Colby's crew stayed overnight and posted footage of flickering shapes and unexplained thumps downstairs. The video racked up millions of views, but skeptics weren't convinced. They pointed to rodents, loose floorboards, and tricks of light.

Cost of Admission

Day tours quickly sold out at $25 per guest; extended paranormal nights climbed to $125 or more. For influencers and content creators, prices went higher, up to $1,500 for exclusive access and filming privileges. Social media buzz made it viral, but some locals grumbled that it had become less haunted house and more haunted amusement park.

An ex-employee, later fired, sued claiming underpayment—and the owner's defense? A 19th-century spirit had accused him of theft. Local skeptics rolled their eyes, calling the operation a "monetary machine wrapped in a haunting." Others worried the site risked historical desecration in the name of entertainment.

The Divided Camp

Within the paranormal community, opinions diverged. Some hailed this as a dream come true: a "living lab" for spiritual investigation. Others saw exploitation—ghost tourism commodifying trauma and fact. One paranormal site even labeled it a "hoax," claiming there was no substantive history before the movie hype began.

Yet visitors kept coming: THE house loomed large in America's haunted lore. Tours were sold out through Halloween season; "ghamping" sold out too—tents full, firewood crackling, nightly whispers of shadowy contacts.

The Thin Line

Still, others adopted a gentler stance. Some saw tourism here as cultural preservation—fueling economic activity in rural Burrillville and drawing attention to colonial-era architecture. Area guides noted that revenue, when handled responsibly, aided historic maintenance and community interest.

"Ghost tourism," a Cornell study noted, could fund preservation—if operators balanced thrill with truth. The Conjuring House offered just that: history,

Hollywood, haunting—a blend of fact and performance.

A Haunted Mirror

Today, the house embodies a paradox: it remains exactly as it was, but means different things to different people:

•A pilgrimage for believers.

•A case study for skeptics.

•A dramatic set for influencers.

•A historical artifact for preservationists.

But for every camper who braves the night, there's someone else fleeing in alarm. For every believer, there's a doubter calling it a prank.

And beneath it all, the house stands silent witness—its halls still holding secrets, its rooms still echoing childhood laughter—and the ghosts of its real past.

SECTION VI:
DEEPER THEMES
& THEORIES

Chapter 20: Why We Believe

It starts with a creak in the floorboards.

A whisper of wind beneath the door.

A light flickering where no draft exists.

And suddenly, the rational mind fumbles.

Even the most grounded person can feel it—that tickle of uncertainty that tiptoes through the dark.

But what if it's not the house that's haunted?

What if it's… us?

The Architecture of Fear

Fear is hardwired. Evolution built it into our bones. The rustle in the bushes could've been the wind—or a predator. Those who assumed danger survived. Those who didn't... didn't.

In today's world, those survival instincts haven't gone away. They've simply shifted. A dim hallway, a late-night thump, a strange feeling when alone—our brains still scan for threats. And when none appear, it fills the silence with stories.

The Pattern Seekers

Humans are pattern-making machines. We seek meaning in randomness, order in chaos. It's called pareidolia—our tendency to see faces in clouds, hear voices in static, or sense presence in an empty room.

At the Conjuring House, visitors often reported hearing a child whisper "Mommy" through EVP. Yet those recordings were often bursts of white noise. The moment you tell someone there's a voice, they hear it.

The mind completes the picture it wants to see—or fears to see.

Primed for the Paranormal

Step into a creaky old house. Now imagine you've been told: A woman died here. They say she still walks the halls.

Suddenly, every creak becomes a footstep. Every flicker—a message.

This is called priming. The brain is told what to expect, and it starts filtering the world through that lens. The Conjuring House, with its legend baked into pop culture, is a perfect petri dish for suggestion. People arrive not wondering if something will happen, but waiting for when it does.

The Stories We Tell Ourselves

Belief in ghosts transcends culture, era, and religion. Ancient Greeks feared spirits wandering the River Styx. In Victorian England, séances became after-dinner entertainment. Today, ghost-hunting shows flood the internet.

But beneath every tale lies a very human question: What happens when we die?

For many, hauntings offer a strange comfort—that something continues, that death isn't final. Even fear can become a form of reassurance. After all, how can we fear being forgotten… if something never leaves?

Confirmation Bias in the Night

Once belief takes root, every experience is judged through its filter.

If you believe a spirit wants to communicate, even a flickering candle becomes a conversation. The brain clings to confirming details and discards the rest. That's confirmation bias—our tendency to interpret new information as evidence for existing beliefs.

The Perrons, living through unexplained events for nearly a decade, didn't invent their terror. But their interpretation of those events was shaped, in part, by belief systems, fear, and environment.

The Need for Mystery

Some scientists argue we believe in hauntings because we can't tolerate randomness. Death, chaos, tragedy— these are hard to accept without meaning. A haunting offers an answer. A narrative. A reason for the unreasonable.

And humans, at their core, are storytellers.

Hauntings Are Human

The Conjuring House, for all its spirits and shadows, is ultimately a mirror. It reflects who we are: seekers, survivors, meaning-makers.

Some believe because they've lived through something that can't be explained. Others believe because the world feels more complete with mysteries in it. And some don't believe at all—yet still feel that shiver when the lights go out.

Perhaps belief isn't a flaw in our minds.

Perhaps it's the soul's way of holding onto wonder.

Chapter 21: The Demon Next Door

The Perron family left the Arnold Estate behind, but something about it stayed with them. Not just the memories or the fear—but a deeper, lingering presence. As Andrea Perron moved into adulthood and later settled in Georgia, she sometimes felt the same heaviness return. It wasn't the same house, nor the same walls. But the feeling was familiar.

There were moments—subtle, passing—when the air in her room felt colder than it should. Her cat would stare at a corner where nothing could be seen. Lights flickered, not always in time with the weather. And sometimes, she would dream—not of ghosts, but of being watched.

It raised the question she couldn't ignore: Do hauntings stay in houses—or can they follow us?

A Haunting That Moves

For centuries, cultures around the world have told stories of spirits that attach themselves to people, not places. Whether called "spirit attachments," "parasites," or simply lost souls, the idea is the same: some entities linger because they're drawn to energy—emotional trauma, grief, guilt, or fear.

Andrea began to wonder if the spirits she encountered as a child weren't confined to the house at all. Maybe, through all those years of fear and curiosity, something had reached out—and latched on.

This wasn't just her imagination. Many survivors of hauntings report similar experiences. Long after they've moved homes or thrown away haunted objects, the disturbances continue. Not the loud, violent kind. But soft knocks. Unexplainable shadows. Dreams that speak.

Residual, Intelligent, or Attached?

In paranormal theory, not all hauntings are created equal. Residual hauntings are like echoes—recordings of the past playing on loop. They don't interact.

Intelligent hauntings, however, are conscious. They respond. They move. They manipulate.

Spirit attachments are something else entirely.

They aren't bound to one house, room, or attic. They stay with a person—often forming a kind of psychic tether. Some say they're drawn to emotional vulnerability. Others believe they're connected to karmic energy or unfinished business.

Andrea, reflecting in later interviews, admitted she wasn't sure which category her family's experience fell into. But she did believe the entity—whatever it was—knew her, recognized her, and remembered.

Unseen Baggage

Stories abound of people carrying attachments unknowingly. One woman moved across the country and began experiencing the same cold spots she had in her childhood home. Another man described waking up each night at exactly 3:07 a.m.—the same time his grandfather died decades earlier.

In many of these accounts, the common thread is emotional trauma. Grief. Unspoken anger. A spiritual weight becomes part of a person's emotional luggage—and sometimes, something else hitches a ride.

Andrea said she often felt emotionally "dragged down" during the anniversaries of certain events—her time in Harrisville, her mother's seance, the last winter before they fled. It was as if the trauma wasn't just a memory, but an active force.

A Shadow by the Door

One night, Andrea stood in her hallway and saw a figure—a blur, a distortion, something there and not there. It vanished the moment she turned her head. She dismissed it at first. But it returned, weeks later, standing in the same place.

No screams. No rattling windows. Just presence. And recognition.

She didn't speak of it often, but when she did, she said she felt pity for the thing. Not fear. "It just wants to be noticed," she told a friend. "It's lonely."

It was then she began to understand: not all spirits want revenge. Some just want release.

Healing the Invisible Thread

Over time, Andrea adopted small rituals of healing. Salt around door frames. A white candle lit before writing. Prayer—not out of fear, but out of respect. She started viewing the experience not as an invasion, but as a connection, however unwanted.

She wrote her books not to trap the story, but to set it free.

Not Just in the House

The Perrons weren't the only family to experience this. Many who've lived in haunted places carry the marks of it long after they leave. It isn't always about a cursed building. Sometimes, the haunting becomes psychological—something planted deep within the subconscious.

But in rare cases, it's more than just memory. It's the presence of something else, walking beside them.

What Follows Us

So are hauntings tied to wood and brick?

Sometimes.

But other times, it's a soul that gets marked. A door that never fully shuts. A bond—created through fear or empathy—that keeps the spirit from moving on.

As Andrea once said: "It may not have followed me. I may have brought it. Or maybe… we both needed each other to let go."

And maybe, the real haunting isn't about a ghost at all. It's about what we carry with us—and what refuses to be forgotten.

Chapter 22: The Conjuring House

Today

Decades have passed since the Perron family's door first swung wide to the Warrens. But time, it seems, does not always still a story—especially not one as storied as the Conjuring House.

1. New Owners, New Stories

In 2023, the Arnold farmhouse stood vacant—weathered wood, sagging shutters, windows dark with dust. That summer, Mark and Priya Kaur, a couple committed to preservation, bought the house not as a haunted attraction, but as a charming historic home. Early on, Mark joked to friends that his greatest renovation fear was "creaking floorboards, not evil spirits." Yet one autumn evening, while repainting an upstairs window frame, he paused, feeling a hush fill the empty room. He heard something—faint, like a child tiptoeing down the hallway—and in that instant, his heart clenched.

Priya encountered oddities too: they installed a motion sensor in the attic that never triggered—until every light flashed just before midnight. Their dogs sometimes froze at the foot of the stairs, staring at a wall behind which no person lurked. They shrugged, blamed house sounds—a settling foundation, maybe mice. But the house didn't settle as quietly as others. And it didn't creep upward without purpose.

2. Modern Investigators

In recent years, ghost hunters—armed with thermal cameras, EMF meters, and binaural recorders—flocked to the property. In one nighttime session, a team captured temperature spikes near the window where Andrea once said she felt a "cold brush of breath." In another, a motion-activated camera filmed a shadow unraveling up the back stairwell. But while believers called it compelling evidence, others pointed out how modern wiring, drafts, and lens flare can mimic mysterious signs.

A visitor from the University of Rhode Island who intended to debunk hauntings ended up unnerved. He left quietly, admitting that seeing his equipment blink unexpectedly, then flicker off when he pointed a light, had left even him unsettled.

Still, no investigation produced conclusive proof—no floating chairs, no unmistakable disembodied voices. What emerged was a patchwork of unnerving moments—not overt terror, but a persisting sense that this house guards its memories carefully.

3. A Cultural Icon

Surrounding the house, the local energy has shifted. What was once a quiet rural stretch on Round Top Road now draws curiosity seekers and film buffs alike.

•Ghost tours operate seasonally, with guides sharing a mix of Perron recollection and cinematic lore.

•A small museum has popped up across the street, displaying Warren artifacts, faded newspaper clippings, and film props.

•YouTube channels frequently post investigations—some earnestly hopeful, others purely entertainment. Lines sometimes blur between homage and hype.

Scholars have taken note. A recent psychology thesis from UMass Boston examined why heritage sites like this house captivate us. It calls the Conjuring House "a bridge between reality and imagination," suggesting that part of its power lies in how it lets us play with both.

4. Quiet as It Remains

Still, those who live nearby have their own long-running view: the haunting isn't in the house—it's in the story. Cameras whir. EVPs hum. Lights flicker. Yet every day the house stands, quiet at its core, carrying echoes of decades past—a container of memory rather than a screaming nexus of supernatural forces.

The Kaur family acknowledges they live with layers of history—some unsettling, some inspiring. They bring coffee to morning quiet and sometimes whisper their own words of welcome to the rooms. At night, they may hear something—but it passes. Or maybe it's theirs to keep.

5. What It Means Today

The Conjuring House isn't just a setting. It's a mirror—in which we examine trauma, storytelling, belief, and wonder.

•It stands for the blend of fact and fiction—and how each shapes the other.

•It embraces our hunger for mystery, balanced against our hunger for truth.

•And it reminds us that while movies end, stories—and the memories they stir—can live on in whispers and half-lights.

This house still speaks. But what it says depends on who listens.

SECTION VII: CLOSURE

Chapter 23: Haunted or Hysteria?

The last light fades from the windows of the old Arnold farmhouse. Night settles once more over the fields of Harrisville. Inside, the stillness returns—except for the quiet creak of a settling floorboard or the murmur of wind through the rafters.

But behind the silence lingers the question that has haunted this story from the beginning:

Was the Conjuring House truly haunted—or was it hysteria, shaped by fear, trauma, and belief?

When the Lights Turn On

Looking back on the Perron family's decade within the house, certain facts stand clear. They endured years of fear—sleepless nights, unexplained phenomena, and a growing tension that nearly broke them. From

Andrea's journals to Carolyn's public statements, their story remained consistent: they believed they lived with something malevolent.

But belief, as the skeptics argue, is not proof.

Electrical issues. Faulty plumbing. Old colonial wood shifting in the night. Exposure to mold, carbon monoxide, or radon gas—all known to create hallucinations, feelings of dread, and even mild cognitive distortion. These are not myths; they are scientifically documented. Could they have played a role?

It's possible. But the Perrons weren't uneducated or hysterical. Carolyn had a background in historical research. Roger worked in land surveying. Andrea was bright, introspective, and articulate. This was not a family prone to fantasy.

So, again, we are left with more questions than answers.

Evidence Collected Over Time

Over the years, numerous paranormal investigators, including the Warrens, visited the house. They recorded voices, captured EMF fluctuations, documented odd temperature shifts. The Warrens conducted a séance that became infamous for its intensity. And modern ghost hunters have returned to find similar anomalies.

Yet none have produced indisputable proof. No verified audio files. No repeatable events under controlled conditions. The best evidence remains deeply personal: eyewitness testimony, unverified recordings, and emotional impressions.

Science demands replication. The supernatural, by its nature, defies it.

What Can't Be Explained

Still, among all the explanations, some events remain hard to dismiss.

•The clocks that stopped at exactly the same time.

•The levitation Carolyn experienced during the séance.

•The bruises that appeared with no cause.

•The disembodied voices—heard by multiple people at once.

•The consistent reports from unrelated visitors who described the same cold spots, the same sounds, and the same sense of dread in the same rooms.

Even skeptical researchers have admitted: something happened in that house. Whether it was supernatural or psychological, its impact was undeniably real.

The House as a Mirror

Perhaps the house was never the source—but a vessel.

A place charged by grief, time, memory, and belief. A crucible where trauma took shape and emotion manifested into story. A place where the past echoed so loudly it felt like the present.

Many hauntings, if not most, begin with emotion. With death. With silence. And then someone hears a sound in the dark—and the human mind does the rest. But sometimes, rarely, there's a sound no one can explain. That's what keeps the doors open.

So, Haunted or Hysteria?

In the end, it may be both.

It may be that the Perrons were caught in a perfect storm of emotional strain, environmental factors, historical resonance, and cultural influence.

It may also be that some places truly hold onto something—energy, intelligence, emotion—something that waits until someone walks in who can feel it.

It may be that the house was haunted.

And it may be that we are all haunted, in our own ways.

The Last Word

The Conjuring House still stands. It still breathes stories. Visitors leave with goosebumps. Believers find proof; skeptics find echoes. But the truth—whatever it is—remains inside those walls, unwilling to leave.

And maybe that's what haunts us most:

Not the ghosts themselves—but the idea that we may never know for sure.

Chapter 24: Legacy of the Perron Haunting

The old farmhouse stands still today—its weathered clapboards and silent rooms a testament to a story that echoes far beyond its walls. But the Perron haunting didn't vanish in 1980. It seeped into our culture, reshaped how we tell ghost stories, and taught other families caution and courage.

Shaping Modern Ghost Lore

When The Conjuring premiered in 2013, grossing over $320□million, it unleashed a wave. People flocked to ghost-hunting shows, EVP forums, and haunted-house tours. The story of a "true haunting" sparked curiosity—and a belief that real ghosts might be out there. Before long, the Perron case had become shorthand for modern fear: a family's trauma woven into Hollywood spectacle, forever blurring lines between history and fiction moleopedia.com+1buggedspace.com+1people.com.

Guiding Other Families Through Fear

When other families experience something strange—a creak, a cold draft, a whisper—they often look to the Perrons as a blueprint. Investigate quietly. Keep records. Speak calmly. Seek help carefully—priest, skeptic, expert, or psychologist. The Perrons didn't flee. They stayed, documented, set boundaries, and kept praying. For many, it's a lesson in measured response over panic.

The Unrelenting Mystery

Decades later, the story still puzzles. Why did a family experience consistent oddities—multiple sisters reporting hearing names, clocks that stopped, plates shifted across tables? Why have unrelated visitors captured similar cold spots? The Conjuring House is now a cautionary tale and a symbol of unexplained wonder.

Modern investigations—skin-crawling infrared shots and EVP whispers—still don't offer a clear answer. Yet the fascination remains, fueled by the idea that mysteries don't always demand resolution.

More Than a Scary Story

The Perrons' ordeal became a cultural lens:

•A case study in collective fear and belief.

•A cautionary template for families navigating unexplained phenomena.

•A symbol of unresolved trauma, at once heartbreaking and universal.

•A cultural icon, inspiring books, documentaries, travel, and film—yet firmly rooted in a 1700s farmhouse in Rhode Island.

An Enduring Enigma

The legacy of the Perron haunting is not its final answers—but its persistence. The house still stands, the world still wonders, and the story keeps pulling us back.

It reminds us of the fragility of belief, the weight of history, and the haunting truth that some stories simply won't let us go.

Epilogue: Faith, Fear, and Forgiveness

The sun sets slowly behind the hills of Harrisville, casting long shadows across the overgrown fields that surround the Arnold Estate. The house stands quiet now—its windows reflecting fading amber light, its doors still, its secrets tucked between floorboards and beams.

But for those who lived within its walls, and for the millions who have followed their story, the house never truly went silent.

It continues to whisper.

A Legacy Etched in Spirit

The Perron family did not ask to become icons of modern paranormal history. They were not thrill-seekers or attention-hungry opportunists. They were a family—imperfect, deeply bonded, and utterly unprepared for what awaited them when they turned the key to that old farmhouse.

They walked in hoping for peace. Instead, they met something else. Something unknowable. Something that took from them more than sleep. It took certainty. It tested love. It pushed belief to its limits.

And yet—they endured.

Faith, Not in Religion Alone

Faith isn't always about God or holy water or stained-glass windows. Sometimes, faith is simply the act of holding each other close in the dark. Of speaking when silence feels safer. Of standing still when every instinct screams to run.

Carolyn Perron's faith was not blind—it was bruised and battered, but resilient. Roger's was built not from religion, but from loyalty. The daughters, each in their own way, clung to the fragile belief that the nightmare would end, that the light would return, and that they'd survive as more than just victims.

Faith, in its truest form, may be nothing more than continuing to love while living through fear.

The Shadow of Fear

Fear changes us. It molds memory. It distorts judgment. But it also sharpens instinct. It makes protectors out of parents, and warriors out of quiet children.

The Perrons knew this intimately.

Their fear taught them caution—but it also taught them resilience. They were scarred, but not broken. And for Andrea, who would grow up to tell the story to the world, the fear became something transformative. A haunting turned into a message. Trauma into testimony.

And Then, Forgiveness

There was no happy ending. The spirits didn't vanish in a final, blinding light. There was no exorcism, no dramatic banishment. The family simply... left. And yet, over time, the rage turned into remembrance. The pain became part of their identity—but it did not define it.

Forgiveness, for them, was not about pardoning a spirit. It was about releasing the bitterness. About refusing to let a house—or what may have lived in it— own their future.

Forgiveness was the last act of power they had. And they chose it.

Why the House Still Matters

To some, the Conjuring House is just wood and stone. To others, it is a portal. To millions more, it's a ghost story told in theaters and whispered between friends. But to the Perrons—and to anyone who has ever felt watched, heard a voice no one else did, or endured what the world refused to believe—it is something more.

It is proof that the veil between the visible and the unseen is thinner than we know.

That fear is real.

That belief is powerful.

And that the human spirit is the most haunting thing of all.

So, is the house still haunted?

Maybe.

Maybe not.

But the story?

That will never rest.

Printed in Dunstable, United Kingdom